READING/WRITING COMPANION

Mc
Graw
Hill
Education

Cover: Nathan Love, Erwin Madrid

mheducation.com/prek-12

Copyright © McGraw-Hill Education

Send all inquiries to:
McGraw-Hill Education
Two Penn Plaza
New York, NY 10121

ISBN: 978-0-07-902059-8
MHID: 0-07-902059-3

Printed in the United States of America.

3 4 5 6 7 8 9 LMN 23 22 21 20 19   C

Welcome to Wonders!

Explore exciting **Literature**, **Science**, and **Social Studies** texts!

★ **READ** about the world around you!

★ **THINK**, **SPEAK**, and **WRITE** about genres!

★ **COLLABORATE** in discussions and inquiry!

★ **EXPRESS** yourself!

my.mheducation.com

Use your student login to read texts and practice phonics, spelling, grammar, and more!

Unit 7 The Animal Kingdom

The Big Idea

Week 1 • Baby Animals

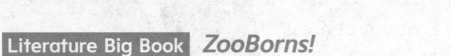

Digital Tools *Find this eBook and other resources at:* **my.mheducation.com**

Week 2 • Pet Pals

Week 3 • Animal Habitats

The Animal Kingdom

The Big Idea

What are different kinds of animals?

 Talk about the different animals in the picture.

 Circle animals in the picture you have seen or read about.

 Describe another animal you know about.

Essential Question How are some animals alike and how are they different?

Talk about how the ducklings and kitten are alike and different.

 Write about how the ducklings and kitten are alike and different.

One way these baby animals are alike is

One way these baby animals are different is

Retell the nonfiction text.

 Write about the text.

One interesting fact I learned is

_____

- -

_____

Text Evidence

Page

_____

- -

_____

One new baby animal name I learned is

 Text Evidence

Page

- -

_____

Talk about baby animals you know.

 Draw and **write** about your favorite baby animal.

My favorite baby animal is

You can compare and contrast when you read. You can think about how things are alike and different.

 Listen to part of the text.

 Compare and **contrast** two of the baby animals.

 Write one way these baby animals are alike and different. Add their names on the lines.

Quick Tip

When we do not understand parts of a text, we can think about what we already know about the topic.

Different   Alike   Different

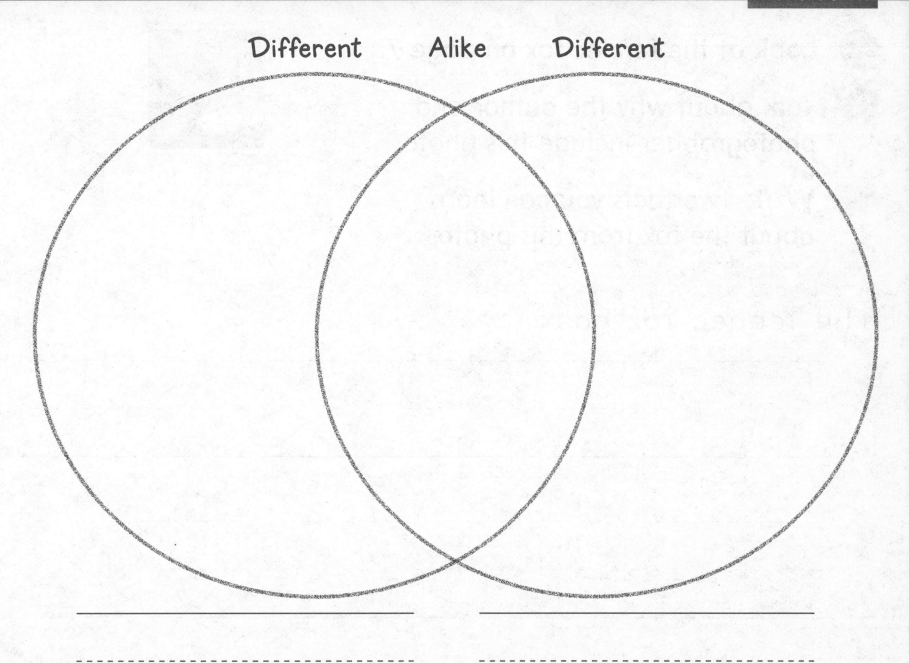

_____   _____

- - - - - - - - - - - - - - - - -   - - - - - - - - - - - - - - - - - -

_____   _____

Look at the fennec fox on page 7.

 Talk about why the author and photographer include this photo.

 Write two facts you can learn about the fox from this photo.

The fennec fox has

_____

1. _____

_____

2. _____

Listen to page 28. Look at the photo.

 Talk about why the author says the wombat's paws are like "built-in shovels."

 Draw and **write** about the wombat's paws.

The wombat's paws

_____

- -

_____

Find Text Evidence

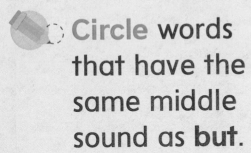 **Read** the title. Look at the photos. Think about what you want to learn from this text.

Circle words that have the same middle sound as **but**.

A Pup and a Cub

I am a pup.

I have a mom and a dad.

🔍 **Find Text Evidence**

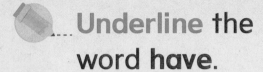 Underline the word **have**.

Draw a box around the animal on page 19 that is not a pet.

I am in a pack.

We sit in a den.

Arco Images/GmbH/Alamy

I am not a pet.

I have not met a pet pup!

Shared Read

 **Find Text Evidence**

Circle words that have the same middle sound as **mud**.

Underline words that tell where the cub on page 21 is.

I am a cub.

Mom and Dad see me.

I sit on a rock in the sun.

I nap in the sun a lot!

Find Text Evidence

Circle words that begin with the same sound as **us**.

Retell the text. Reread if you do not understand something.

Sis and I have fun.

We can go up, up!

Aditya Singh/Moment Open/Getty Images

A pup can run for fun.

A cub can run for fun.

Listen to "Over in the Meadow." Which words in the poem rhyme?

 Draw the word that rhymes with **one**.

 Write the word.

Quick Tip

We can add to the poem by thinking of new actions that baby animals can do.

"We (swim/jump/fly)," said the ____.

The word that rhymes with **one** is

Listen to the poem.

 Circle the animals Kitty did catch.

 Draw a box around the animal that Kitty did not catch.

 Write About It

Use this pattern to write a new verse for the poem.

Kitty caught a ___.

Kitty did not catch a ___.

Animal Features

Step 1 Talk about animals and their special features. Choose one to learn about.

Step 2 Write a question about how your animal uses its special feature.

_____

- -

_____

- -

_____

Step 3 Look at books or use the Internet.
Look up words you do not know.
Use a picture dictionary.

Step 4 **Draw** and **write** about what you learned.

Step 5 **Choose** a good way to present your work.

 Talk about these animals. How are they alike? How are they different?

 Compare these animals to the animals in *ZooBorns!*

Quick Tip

To help us **compare** and **contrast**, we can look for details in pictures.

What I Know Now

Think about the texts you read this week.

The texts tell about

_____

- -

_____

_____

- -

_____

 Think about what you learned this week.
What else would you like to learn?
Talk about your ideas.

 Share one thing you learned
about nonfiction texts.

Talk About It

Talk about how this boy takes care of his dog.

 Draw and **write** about one way you would take care of a dog.

I would take care of a dog by

THEPALMER/E+/Getty Images

Retell the realistic fiction story.

Write about the story.

Danny wants a turtle because

 Text Evidence

Page

This is realistic fiction because

 Text Evidence

Page

Talk about a pet you would like to get.

 Draw and **write** about why you would want this pet.

I would want this pet because

_____

- -

_____

Most stories have a problem and a solution.

- **The problem is what a character wants to do or fix.**

- **The way the character solves the problem is the solution.**

 Listen carefully to part of the story.

 Talk and **write** about Danny's problem.

Draw and **write** about the solution.

The solution is

_____

- -

_____

Listen for rhyming words on pages 11–12. What word helps you predict Danny's next pet?

 Talk about how the two words are alike.

 Draw both words.

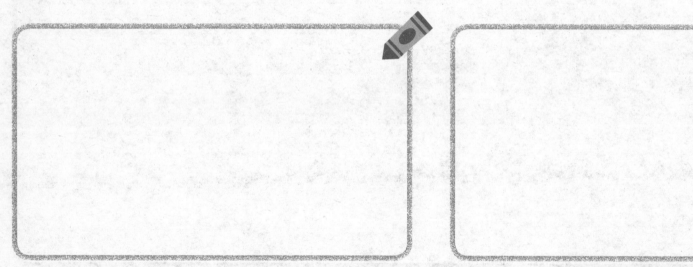

Quick Tip

The **rhyming words** in the story can help us to predict what pet will come next.

Look at pages 24–25.

 Talk about how Danny feels about the turtle.

 Draw and **write** about how he feels.

Danny feels

_____

- -

_____

Find Text Evidence

I Hug Gus!

Read the title. Look at the pictures. Think about what you want to find out in this story.

Circle words that end with the same sound as **tag**.

I can see a big, red pup.

I pick a pup for a pet.

Shared Read

Underline the word **They**.

Circle who can run, run, and win!

My big pup and a cat tug.

They tug and have fun.

Gus is a big, red pup.

Gus can run, run, and win!

🔍 **Find Text Evidence**

🖊️ **Underline** the word **of**.

🖊️ **Circle** two rhyming words.

Gus is on top of the bed.

He can sit up and beg.

Gus and I are on a rug.

Gus can tug, tug, tug!

 **Find Text Evidence**

Circle words that begin with the same sound as **get**.

Retell the story in order. Use the words and pictures to help you with parts you do not understand.

I rub Gus in the tub.

Gus is wet, wet, wet!

I tuck Gus in a big bed.

I can hug, hug, hug Gus!

Listen to the personal narrative.

 **Circle** the character who is telling the story. Write her name.

 Talk about words that help you know the author is telling the story about herself.

Quick Tip

Authors sometimes write about events that happened in their lives. This kind of story is called a **personal narrative**.

Listen to pages 34–35. How does Lola use sound words to make her story come to life?

 Draw and **write** about Bella making a sound.

Write About It

Lola wrote about herself and a pet. Now write a personal narrative about yourself and a pet you have or know. Include sound words.

The sound Bella makes is

_____

- - - - - - - - - - - - - - - - - - - -

_____

Caring for a Pet

Step 1 **Talk** about how you would care for different pets. Choose one pet to learn about.

Step 2 **Write** a question about how to care for this pet.

_____

- -

_____

_____

- -

_____

Step 3 **Look** at books or use the Internet. Look up words you do not know. Use a picture dictionary.

Step 4 Draw what you learned.

Step 5 Write about what you learned
in your writer's notebook. Use new words
that you learned.

Step 6 Choose a good way to present your work.

Make Connections

 Talk about the photo.
What clues tell you how this girl feels about her pet rabbit?

 Compare this girl and her rabbit to Danny and his turtle in *The Birthday Pet*.

Quick Tip

To talk about the photo, we can say:

The girl loves her rabbit because ____.

The rabbit looks ____.

Claudia Rehm, Red Chopsticks Images/Getty Images

What I Know Now

Think about the texts you read this week.

The texts tell about

_____

- -

_____

- -

_____

 Think about what you learned this week.
What else would you like to learn?
Talk about your ideas.

 Share one thing you learned
about realistic fiction stories.

Talk About It

Essential Question **Where do animals live?**

Talk about the photo. Why is the den a good home for the fox?

 Draw and **write** about an animal home you know.

This is a good home because

_____

_____

Respond to the Big Book

Bear Snores On

Retell the fantasy story.

Write about the fantasy.

In Bear's den, the animals

Text Evidence

Page

I know this is a fantasy because

Text Evidence

Page

Talk about what real animals do in the winter.

 Draw and **write** about a real animal in the winter.

In winter, _____

- -

_____

A **cause** is what makes something happen in a story. An **effect** is the event that happens.

 Listen to pages 8–9.

 Talk about what causes Mouse to go in the cave.

 Write about the cause and effect.

The weather is

_____

- -

This causes Mouse to

_____

- -

_____

Listen to pages 24–26.
What causes Bear to wake up?

 Draw the cause and effect.

Listen to pages 24–26.

Quick Tip

To find the **effect**, ask: *What happens?* To find the **cause**, ask: *What makes it happen?*

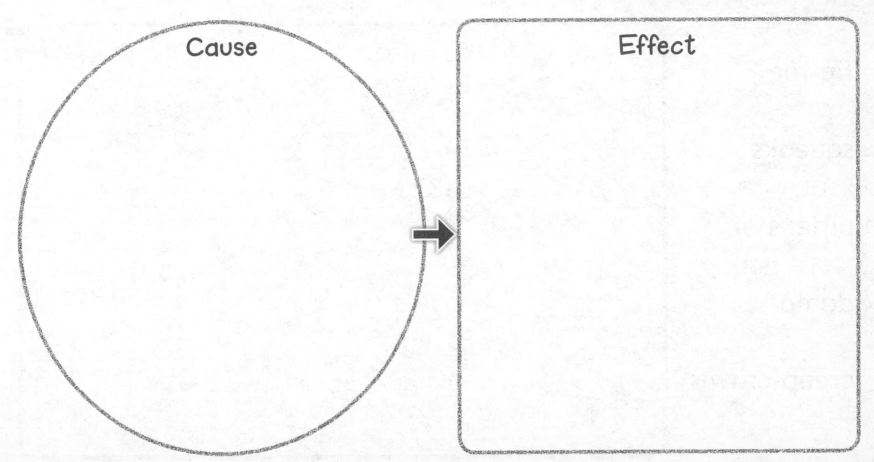

Cause

Effect

Big Book

 Listen to pages 8–9.
The events begin in a quiet way.
Which words help you picture this?

 Circle the words.

 Draw a picture.

tip-toe

squeaks

pitter-pat

damp

creep-crawls

Listen to pages 32–34.

 Talk about the end of the story. Why do you think the author ends the story this way?

 Draw and **write** about it.

 Combine Information

Talk about the pattern in this story. What changes inside the cave? What stays the same?

At the end of the story,

_____

- -

_____

Find Text Evidence

Make a prediction about the story. Use the title and pictures to help you. Read to find out if your prediction is correct.

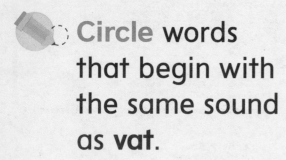
Circle words that begin with the same sound as **vat**.

A Vet in a Van

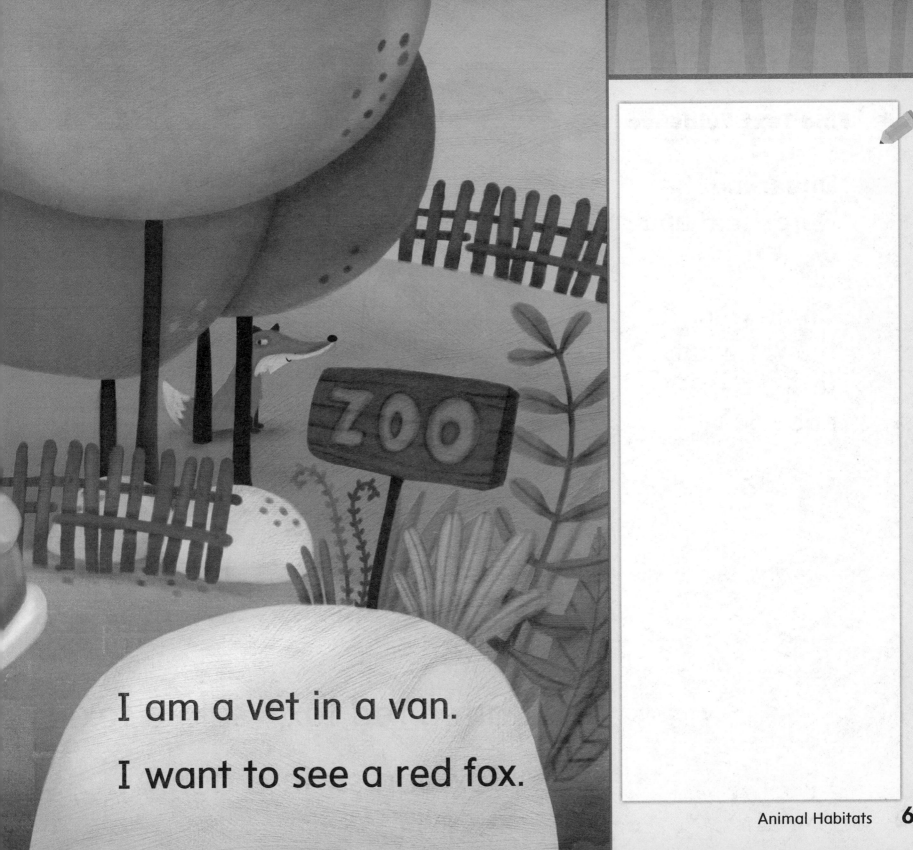

I am a vet in a van.

I want to see a red fox.

🔍 **Find Text Evidence**

✏️ **Underline** the words **said** and **want**.

✏️ **Circle** who the vet wants to see on page 63.

"I am a red fox," said a fox.

"A fox can sit in a den."

I want to see a big cat.

I can go in my van.

Shared Read

 Find Text Evidence

 Think about what has happened so far. Make a prediction about what will happen. Read on to see if your prediction is correct.

Circle the picture that shows **six**.

"I am a big cat," said a cat.

"I can sit on a rock."

I can see a pig.

I can see six!

Shared Read

🔍 **Find Text Evidence**

 Circle words that end with the same sounds as **box**.

Talk about your prediction. Was it correct? Use the words and pictures to help you decide. Then retell the story.

I see a sick ox.

I can fix a bad leg.

"I met a vet!" said the ox.

"A vet can fix a sick ox!"

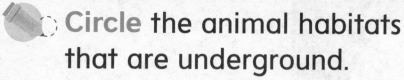 **Look** at the animal habitats.
How are they alike and different?

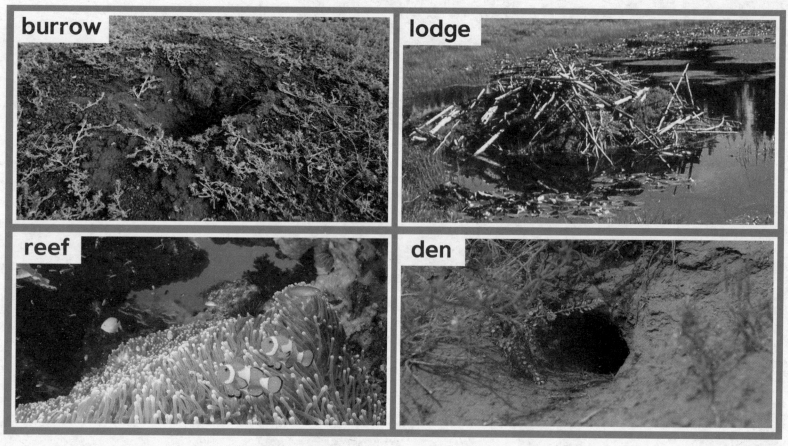

burrow

lodge

reef

den

Circle the animal habitats
that are underground.

Draw boxes around the habitats
that are in the water.

Look at page 38. What does the author want you to know?

Write about it.

The small picture shows

_____

- -

_____

The label tells

_____

- -

_____

The photo shows

_____

- -

_____

Quick Tip

To talk about animal habitats, we can say:

This animal lives in a ___.

It is a good habitat because ___.

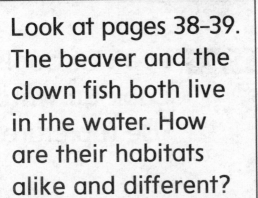

Talk About It

Look at pages 38–39. The beaver and the clown fish both live in the water. How are their habitats alike and different?

Animal Habitats

Step 1 Talk about animal habitats.
Choose one to learn about.

Step 2 Write a question about the habitat.

_____

- -

_____

_____

- -

_____

Step 3 Look at books or use the Internet.
Look up words you do not know.
Use a picture dictionary.

Step 4 Draw what you learned.

Step 5 Write about what you learned
in your writer's notebook. Use new words
that you learned.

Step 6 Choose a good way to present your work.

Talk about the photo.

A meerkat mother and pup look out of their burrow.

 Compare the meerkat habitat with Bear's habitat in *Bear Snores On.*

Quick Tip

To talk about animal habitats, we can say:

Animals live together in a ___ (meadow, desert, ocean, forest, pond, jungle).

Jonathan Heger/E+/Getty Images

What I Know Now

Think about the texts you read this week.

The texts tell about

_____

- -

_____

- -

_____

_____

 Think about what you learned this week.
What else would you like to learn?
Talk about your ideas.

 Share one thing you learned
about fantasy stories.

My Sound-Spellings

Aa — a — apple

Bb — b — bat

Cc — c ck k — camel

Dd — d — dolphin

Ee — e — egg

Ff — f — fire

Gg — g — guitar

Hh — h_ — hippo

Ii — i — insect

Jj — j — jump

Kk — c k ck — koala

Ll — l — lemon

Mm — m — map

Nn — n — nest

Oo — o — octopus

Pp — p — piano

Qq — qu_ — queen

Rr — r — rose

Ss — s — sun

Tt — t — turtle

Uu — u — umbrella

Vv — v — volcano

Ww — w_ — window

Xx — x — box

Yy — y_ — yo-yo

Zz — z _s — zipper

Aa Bb Cc Dd Ee

Ff Gg Hh Ii Jj

Kk Ll Mm Nn

Oo Pp Qq Rr

Ss Tt Uu Vv

Ww Xx Yy Zz